10 Items Or Less- 50 Years On The Express Line

John Terlato

Published by John Terlato, 2023.

While every precaution has been taken in the preparation of this book, the publisher assumes no responsibility for errors or omissions, or for damages resulting from the use of the information contained herein.

10 ITEMS OR LESS- 50 YEARS ON THE EXPRESS LINE

First edition. April 10, 2023.

Copyright © 2023 John Terlato.

ISBN: 979-8215876992

Written by John Terlato.

Table of Contents

For all the people that make retail what it really is...you know
who you are and you know what it is!

10 Items Or Less
50 Years On The Express Line
By John Terlato

For all the people that make retail what it really is...you know who you are

and you know what it is.

Only some names were changed to protect the guilty

"There is no need for exaggeration as life provides"

John Calada 2023

Table Of Contents

Chapter 1-Off And Running

So yesterday was my High School graduation. Class of '72. Four horrible years of wishing I stayed home coming right off the heels of two horrible years of Junior High. Not to be left out, but the previous seven years were equally as horrible. I was comfortable at home. I had my books,art,hobbies, and of course television. Since my family upgraded to a color TV, my life felt complete. During the aforementioned seven years, it is worth telling that those years were spent in the parochial system of New York State. I came out of that program ready for the world and ready to accept any beating from anybody. The nuns that ran the school were all former WWE wrestlers, or so it seemed. They literally beat religion into me.My experiences there could provide me with a sequel down the road. So yesterday was graduation day. A hot summer Sunday surrounded by family and a handful of friends I had made over the years. I would have rather been home! Needless to say I was not the type of student to get involved with after school activities. My typical school schedule was 8a.m to 2:30p.m. I was home at 2:31! No clubs. No sports, This reflected in my yearbook photo with nothing attributed to me beneath my picture. If lying on the couch in my parents living room was a sport, I would have been All State! Eighteen years of television. Ask me anything. I became a trivia expert in the field of 60's T.V. Graduation was full of inspiring speeches and testimonials from successful alumni. They painted many pictures of a glorious future in the hot June sun. A wave of motivation and hope swept over the crowd. Everyone seemed to have plans and dreams. Everyone seemed to have scholarship funding to help with those plans. Waking up at home on Monday morning, still reeling from the fact that school was forever over, I began to plan my summer of relaxation. I turned to my best friend, the couch. Good to see you old friend. Allow me to sit. To think. To plan. To reach for the remote.I proceed to lay down,get comfortable,and begin to live the rest of my life right here. Something was breaking the silence. The dogs are barking as the front door bell incessantly rang.Why now? At the beginning of my adult life I am being interrupted. I realized I would have to react to this or I would not get my well deserved rest. As I opened the door, I was surprised to see my Neighbor, Norman. He was standing there in a loud colorful business suit which was set off beautifully against his glowing spray tanned skin.His hair was perfectly landscaped into a 70's pop star look and his equally colorful tie was wider than myself. I had never really spoken to him as he was closer in age with my parents and had more in common with them than with me. I felt intimidated meeting with him one on one. "Hi John. Congratulations on graduating. I am here to offer you a position with my company. They are hiring for the summer and thought you might be interested.You would have to act fast as these positions are being filled." Wait a minute, Did he say "act fast", Me? This was a situation I have never encountered. Norman worked as a supervisor for a very successful supermarket chain based largely on Long Island. This company was a household word. Norman explained to me that I would have to travel to the next town and meet with the store manager to fill out the application. My head was spinning. Do I want to do this? This changes everything.Do I want this responsibility, sign a contract to show up on time. Have a weekly schedule. A job! I haven't spent enough time putting a pessimistic spin on this. At this I am also an All Star. Before I knew it , I was one town over, meeting with the manager. Frank was a grandfatherly figure who seemed to be doing this because Norman told him to. Good start! Frank could care less. The fact that I had a pulse was good enough for him. He offered me a part time position as a grocery clerk. I would be making minimum wage, working nights and weekends, and not to forget holidays. The speakers at graduation were right. The world was my oyster. I was put on the schedule for a whopping 19 hours which included an 8 hour shift on Saturday. 8hours! Are you serious? School was only 6 ½. How could I stay away from the house for 8 hours? Somebody help!

Chapter 2-Breaking The Ice

My first day, or should I say night. I climbed into my $300 graduation money acquired vehicle. My 1960 Chevy Impala.The eight track player was cranking classic rock as I drove to the store through squinting eyes. I didn't know what to expect. First job. Strangers. Not a fan of meeting new people or any people for that matter.I pull into the parking lot and step forward towards my future. After stumbling through the first day protocol, I was introduced to the members of the crew. In those days, payroll must not have been an issue as there were about 15 grocery guys arriving at the same time as me. We all assembled in the stockroom where the ritual began. An enormous amount of stock was waiting for us after being delivered earlier in the day. Each crew member had an assigned aisle or two to stock. The boxes were in no particular order as they were stacked on the floor of the stockroom. It was the crew members responsibility to sort and load through this mountain, making sure to take every case destined for their aisles. The stock was built up on a cart and rolled onto the sales floor. Once there, the stock had to be priced and packed onto the shelves. After all the cases were stocked out, the empty cardboard had to be taken to the stockroom to be baled. The cases were thrown into a large machine which would then crush the cardboard into a flattened bale. The next step in the process was to return to the aisle and fashion the shelves into a "grand opening" look. Bottles were pulled forward and cans were leveled down giving the entire aisle a polished, finished look. Shopping cart round-up came next. All the carts were collected from the parking lot and rolled into the store. To complete the evening, the floors throughout the entire store needed to be swept,mopped,and waxed. We had the luxury of a floor machine for the waxing but the rest was done by hand with mops and brooms. All this work in the space of 5 hours. All this work for minimum wage. This was a lot to grasp at first. The crew seemed a bit standoffish so I shadowed the Grocery Manager in an attempt to try and understand the processes. He had begun to cut open a case and price some cans. I noticed he was able to do both with amazing speed. When I expressed how fast he was at this job, he spoke the words that I would never forget. "After nine years of doing this, you will be this fast at pricing". Nine years! Yeah right! I was laughing inside thinking I would be here nine years from now. This industry was not what I saw myself getting involved in.Oh, little did I know! As the night progressed into weeks, then months,I was still taking my union breaks by myself. Sitting in the Chevy, listening to the classics, and surviving on egg rolls and iced tea. The other fifteen teammates would all break together, walk to Mickey D's and extend a 15 minute break into an hour. I was back in record time. Finally I was approached by one of the veteran crew members. Older guy. Respected. He asked me about my Uncle Norm. "So your Uncle Norman got you this job?" They all assumed I was a spy, planted in the store,to report back to my neighbor Norman! If that was the case. I would hope to be hired at more than minimum. I set the story straight. All was well. I guess this is where my story really begins.

Chapter 3- An Early Promotion...Of Sorts

Apparently I was doing well enough in the grocery department to be selected to help close the dairy. I felt good about being the one chosen out of the fifteen of us. Each department had its own manager. Big money managers as I later found out. The dairy had Mr. Frank Bosco. He would leave as soon as I came in .He was a stereotypical 70's male.The hair. The clothes.The car. Frank didn't notice that I was there as he continued to flirt with a female customer who was shopping with a friend. He was ready to leave as he was wearing a leather trench coat and spinning his Ferrari key ring around on his finger. As he smiled, it seemed to cast a light from his teeth onto his lady friend. Not realizing I could hear his every word, Frank began to lay out his plan to meet theTWO ladies at the motel down the street. As they headed towards their car, Frank began to pile on more work than I could handle in a four hour shift. He, clearly, wasn't thinking straight. He did mention milk and leveling so I went with that. Milk, in those days, was delivered in large metal crates.You would be able to stack the crates once they were empty. Soon you would be surrounded by stacks of empty crates in the aisle. This night is when I found out that my prestigious position in dairy was actually looked at as a demotion. You were, in a sense, cast out of grocery and were on your own. The term "dairy fairy" was being thrown around alot on this particular night and I was not in the mood. As the teasing from the next aisle increased, I retaliated and hurled one of the crates over the top of the aisle hoping to cripple at least one of the grocery guys. As luck would have it, said crate narrowly missed a female shopper and ended up in her shopping cart. The grocery crew came to my rescue as they all pointed in the opposite direction of the projectile and I was able to escape into the backroom. This display of bravado on my part enabled me to ascend to the heights of finally being accepted. Also, the fact that the crew thought I was insane did not hurt my reputation.

Chapter 4- Lasting Impressions

The other department managers read like a casting list for a very bad sitcom. These are the people we aspire to be? Overweight, over stressed,smelly middle aged men apparently knowledgeable enough to hold a management position. All except Frank in the dairy, god knows! The key to successful management seemed to be owning a grotesque collection of wide neckties. These, when worn in conjunction with patterned shirts,would definitely get someone noticed. Khaki pants and worn shoes would complete the look of a true professional. Some of these fashion trends could be chalked up to it being the 70's, but still hideous. These were the role models of a largely staffed teenage workforce. The work force consisted of rebels and wise guys who went out of their way to question authority. Let's face it, we all realized this was not the future for many of us to take it seriously. This was a part time job, to collect a paycheck, hang out with your buddies,and meet girls. Let me begin by introducing some of these rebels. Bob, senior man on the grocery crew. He was able to survive 4 years and had earned the respect of the management team. He was finishing up in college and had the bosses snowballed.He more or less took the rookies under his wing. Bob's cousin, Patrick, was also in school. He was destined for greatness as an educator and simply did not belong here. Mike was heading out the door to pursue being a CPA. Joe, right off the boat from Italy, was a calming influence on the crew. Joe would only get upset when customers mispronounced Italian products. Do not ask him where the "zitty" was. Timmy and Mel were seasoned veterans and worked as a team. Mel would chain smoke cigarettes in the aisle all day long. Memorable! Tim provided the "hippie vibe" with his uncaring attitude.Speaking of hippies,let me focus on Bob Costello. Oh my god! Shoulder length blonde hair growing out of a huge bald area on the very top of his head. He wore little John Lennon glasses that were perched on the end of his long needle pointed nose. Bob had been married for a short time but it ended in mass quantities of weed to help him cope with it. The entire time Bob worked with us, no one can remember him being straight for one single day. Most of his paycheck was spent on alimony and weed and we assumed he was living out of his van.He used the van to set up a lunchtime concert hall in the parking lot. He would take the tower speakers from the van and set them on the ground. He cranked his music to 11 and spent the next hour smoking bowl after bowl of the worst weed on the planet. Pure garbage, I guess the price was right. He had amassed gallon glass jars full of this crap that were stored on shelves in the van. One day, during the concert, 15 police cars came screaming into the parking lot. Lights and sirens. Bob panicked and started unscrewing the lids on his stash. He opened a window and started pouring the weed onto the ground. It turned out that the police were using our parking lot as a shortcut to the bypass behind us. When Bob realized the police were not going to stop because of him, he panicked again. He jumped out of the van and started to rescue his weed. Between the wind and the fact that he could only pick up a little at a time, he gave up. Bad day for Bob. Another bad day comes to mind. The crew spent a lot of time relaxing on the front window ledge of the store. We were located in a stirp mall,one of many on Long Island,and had a lot of foot traffic in both directions. We would spend breaks,lunch,and any opportunity to goof off on the ledge. The ledge also played a part in our Friday night boys night out. We would all head to the ledge after bar hopping and diner hopping,waiting for the opening manager to let us in when the sun came up. Yes, we hardly ever went home. This one summer day, we were on the ledge for no specific reason. We noticed two women walking towards the store. One of the women was very curvy and very braless. Bob was beside himself. He stared so hard that he actually raised up off the bench as they got closer. Bob began to whimper. She smiled at him and while juggling her breasts in her hands asked the pointed question "Do you like what you see?". Bob became catatonic and used his goofy smile to shake his head yes. She continued walking and juggling"More bounce to the ounce!". We almost called an ambulance for Bob but he settled back on the ledge and watched the women enter the store.Our break was over so we all rose as one and went back to work. The ladies had disappeared into the maze of aisles and we lost sight of them. We went about our business and entered the backroom. While assembling our work loads, we notice one of the managers and a strange man looking through the window on the stockroom door. I see the manager point and the door swing open to reveal a very large,very irate man. The man yelled out "That's him!" and pointed at Bob. For some reason we all formed a circle assuming a fight was about to break out. At this point, the manager asked a simple question" Bob, were you rude to this man's wife?" to which Bob simply answered " I guess I was...but if that was my wife I wouldn't be proud of it!" The man had to be restrained and was professionally escorted out of the store. Bomb defused. Back to work. Amazing how Bob never apologized or was asked to apologize. Oh, the seventies,

Chapter 5-Fat Joe

Now that you met the starting line up, The guys I've spent ten years of my life with, here comes the ringer. We were all in our late teens or early twenties. They hired a new 'boy', Fat Joe, as he was affectionately referred to. Joe was 48 years old, single for obvious reasons,and had risen to the lofty heights as a stock boy. He was a friend of a friend who was hired full time. Hygiene was not Joe's strong suit. He lived with his dad above a deli in a neighboring town. He smelled of deli.He was not able to tuck in his shirts, again for obvious reasons, and wore ties similar to Oliver Hardy. The most notable characteristic about Joe was that,no matter the situation, when need be, he would not only pick his nose in full view of everyone but would eat whatever he dug out. This was commonplace for Joe, In the middle of the morning huddle. Meeting with supervision. Weekly meetings. No boundaries. The turning point for me was when Joe was selected to make the morning breakfast run for the crew. I would pass on this morning ritual going forward.Joe stayed with us longer than predicted. He continued to make our gatherings more colorful with his finger buried in his nose. The deli smell must have kept everyone hungry for most of the day. One day Joe was gone. Didn't ask.Didn't care.Maybe he died or moved on to work with Greenpeace.Emphasis on the"green"!

Chapter 6-Just Being A Young Adult

So being the late bloomer in every category up until now,the crew opened up many new doors for me. My first drink was a pitcher of dark beer I had grabbed off a table at a store party. After throwing up on the hood of a Corvette parked outside the door, this was my last experience with dark beer. Hot rods, clubs and dating were new and exciting worlds to explore. I fell in with the car guys due to the extraordinary amount of bolt ons added to my second car,the Ford Galaxy. I might mention I had totaled the Impala during a minimal snow storm. After I slid into a telephone pole at 30 mph, the car was left on the avenue while I phoned my dad. Upon returning, I noticed five more cars had been involved with my Impala leaving it a crumpled mess of metal. As dad arrived to save the day from my minor accident, all I could see was him shaking his head slowly as he made his way past the array of emergency vehicles and ambulances. Good times! The Hot Rod guys were impressed with the Ford. It was raised in the back to allow me to add the widest tires I could fit in the well. Aluminum rims and a killer sound system, for its time, added to the coolness. This car meant everything to me at the time. I invested 99% of my weekly pay into this project. I finally got up the nerve to start speaking to one of the more popular cashiers. She had asked me to give her a ride home after work. I couldn't believe this was happening. I told her to meet me outside after our shifts were over. She climbed into the car and as I pulled into traffic on the busy bypass, I was quickly shut down by a red light. This is when she turned to me and said "Wow,this car is some piece of shit!". Hoping I heard her wrong, I was clearing my head when she repeated the entire sentence word for word. Without thinking, I reached across her and flung open the passenger door. "Get out of my car!" She began to hope she had heard wrong and said "Excuse me!" I repeated "Get out!" over and over until she did. I left her standing in the middle of one of the busiest intersections on Long Island. She was afraid to move. When the light turned green, I screeched the tires and only looked back once to see her still standing in the same spot. This relationship went nowhere after that. The crew loved the story. Italian Joe showed up in a stereotypical Fiat Spyder. Dairy Doug surprised everyone with his 73 Duster. CPA Mike never moved up from his dads 'hand me down Nova. This phenomena quickly spread to the neighborhoods. My childhood friends were all driving monsters.My best friend,Mike,from High School had an awesome looking, yet piece of crap, Pontiac Firebird.It was fun and expensive. It became a competition.Many of the dads were reliving their glory days and also got involved in their kids projects. Now we all had cars! Time to cruise!

Chapter 7-The Faces

The biggest rite of passage was the evolution of dating. It was kind of sad that the crew all found girlfriends in the store. Captive audience syndrome perhaps. This was like an experimental marriage where you would have to account for every move and every word spoken. Forget about making plans with your friends and sticking to them. This was a whole new world. Not one of us did any research in this field before diving in head first. I fell prey to the relationship frenzy but did not confine myself to one girl. I know, scummy, but what was a nineteen year old with a cool car supposed to do? Friday nights became "Boys Night Out". We needed to regroup and find ourselves once more. We were all of drinking age and had wheels.We would spend the entire night hopping from one club to another in the space of five miles. The clubs were everywhere and Disco was just born. It's easy to compare these times with Saturday Night Fever. We were the faces, depending on what club we were in. We tried to out drink each other and flirted with every girl we could. Some of us could actually dance! The girlfriends decided they would not sit idly by while we were having the times of our lives without them. They decided they would also go out, as a group, on Friday night. The ground rules were simple. We agreed not to go to the same bars. We would have an agenda meeting during the day on Friday establishing the boundaries. All was working fine for the first few weeks, We would stay on the north side of the avenue and the girls would stay south. We would stay out all night, hit the diner at about 3am. and make our way back to the ledge. It was always a surprise for the opening manager to see us waiting, all dressed up from the night before, reporting to work. The best part was that only the better crew members would be allowed to work on Saturday. This was status! To be left off the schedule was a clear sign that you should seek employment elsewhere. So here we were, the cream of the crop,tired and hung over. Nauseous from the diner food.We invented a new challenge. We would bet on which of the crew would end up going home sick. Looking back, this is where the term "sucker bet' was born. Good times! There was a time when worlds collided. Firebird Mike and I arrived at one of the northern clubs ahead of everyone else. As we walked in, Mike was greeted by the sight of his fiance sitting on some guy's lap. In one of the smoothest moves ever, he walked towards her and gave her a cute little wave. He was wiggling his fingers with a big smile on his face. He then turned towards the door and I followed in disbelief of what I just witnessed. We went back to the car which he started with a tremendous roar. As he was revving the engine he turned to me and asked for a cigarette. No big deal. It's just that he didn't smoke. He lit up and continued to rev his engine.

"What are we gonna do now?" I asked. He threw the cigarette butt out the window. "Now we wait. I know she will be running out here to try and explain"' I thought to myself that he was handling this too well. He shifted the car into drive as she came bursting through the double doors of the bar. Mike looked at me and calmly said "Now I'll run her down"! The car screeched sideways narrowly missing her. I opened my eyes, after what seemed like a long time, and realizing that he missed felt relieved. This was not the only time that he threatened to kill her. I remember three more! Not to worry, she is still alive and they are still together after forty years. I miss Mike! The Friday night rules were still in place after this incident. Mike no longer joined us.Not sure whose decision that was. Many stories exist about these legendary Friday nights. The later it became, ladies became more drunk and we all looked a lot better to them. We would meet and sometimes arrange a second meeting with some of these ladies. The members of the crew needed proof that any of this was true so another game was invented. Anyone could say they met a fantastic woman after everyone went home. Let the games begin!

Chapter 8-You Needed Proof...You Got It!

The problem was not only cheating on your girl back at the store, but proving to your buddies that some miracle took place after they went home. Simple solution. Invite the girl you met the night before to come to the store and meet you for lunch on Saturday. This would be all the proof you needed that the girl existed .All you had to do was avoid the girlfriend working up front and head out to Burger King. The best example of how this plan was foolproof came out of meeting an adult magazine centerfold at three in the morning . Asking the guys to accept a lot here! She was drunk and stumbled into me spilling my drink. I was annoyed and insisted she buy me a drink to replace the one she spilled. We spent some time talking and at the end I realized this had to be a Saturday lunch date. At around noon on Saturday, I saw and heard the crew following a young lady from aisle to aisle in the store. The crowd grew as word of this amazing creature was in the store. She was taller than I remembered with waist length red hair. She had on a midriff shirt tied in the middle that was barely containing her breasts. Being winter, she was also wearing a full length fur coat and thigh high boots. When she stopped one of the boys and asked for me, you could hear the jaws dropping on the floor. We snuck out the door and began to drive to the King when I noticed the entire crew following us. The table I chose was quickly surrounded by the boys as they pulled adjoining tables close.None of them ordered food, they just stared. I win! The relationship never got past this day as she was also involved with her business manager. One day was good enough for me. As I think back, there were never any other contestants involved in this game.

Chapter 9-Cruisin' and Bruisin'

With the many cars in our club came many stories. Weekday nights were slated for illegal drag racing on one of the more popular county routes. The police were aware of this but didn't enforce the law unless things got out of hand. Hundreds of people lined the streets as this 5 mile stretch of road was the place to be. As the traffic lights turned from red to green, you could hear the squeal of tires signifying a race was on. Some of the racers did this for a living by winning money and even the opponents car.The route was made up of many fast food restaurants, clubs, and ironically late night auto parts stores. Street vendors worked the crowd selling anything from snacks to clothing paying homage to the beloved route. T-shirts, sweatshirts, and posters were sold by the vendors. Many races ended with name calling and fist fights as betting was the underlying factor in all these instances. As the crew made their way to the route,three towns away, they all had hopes of their car being a crowd pleaser. The onlookers would cheer for an exciting car as it rolled by. We never raced for money. We went to mostly show off.Depending on the crowd, some cheered while others booed.

We would cruise together pretending to be interested in breaking some laws. We rarely got involved.These nights would provide some great stories back at the store. With so many boys' nights, it was a wonder why the girls put up with this. At one point during the night, the pretending became all too real. A car full of thugs pulled up next to us and expected to race. We ignored them and cruised towards a place to stop and eat. As we pulled into the drive thru lane, we were met with the headlights from the thugs car as they entered through the exit. These guys were serious. Headlights to headlights as

The occupants of the car began to scream obscenities at us and hurl garbage. It is surprising how well you can speed in reverse. We escaped, momentarily, and got back on the road.A chase ensued lasting the length of the next two towns over. I remembered where we were and also remembered there were train tracks we needed to cross. At top speed, we noticed the guard rail lights pop on as the gate began to close. Should we rethink our escape plan was the question on everybody's mind. Hell no! At full speed, the Buick Skylark slipped under the closing gate and hurtled over the tracks becoming airborne for a few seconds.As the car landed we realized we had escaped as we left the punks on the other side of the tracks. A leisurely drive home consisting of high fives and sighs of relief awaited us. As we pulled into my buddy John's driveway, so did the thugs. This night is not over. The only saving grace was John's dad, all five feet of him, running out of the house swinging a bat in the air.To our surprise the other car hauled ass. Good times!

Chapter 10-Good Vibrations

Summer had arrived! The quest for full time hours began. There was a considerable raise involved from going to a part time to full time employee. The only positions that were left for any of us was to work the overnight shift. This involved many of the portering duties which included washing and waxing the floors, cleaning the restrooms, gathering the trash, and if you had any time after all that, prepping some departments for the morning customers. We had to work in the produce department wrapping lettuce, dairy filling milk and eggs, and bagging bread for sale.Fortunately most of the crew was willing to work this shift along with myself. We were efficient to a fault. We had also managed to talk a culinary student into working with us. His main job was feeding us. The menu varied night by night. The first course consisted of a fresh salad prepared in a brand new, never used, 55 gallon garbage pail. Entrees ranged from many cuts of meat,appropriated off the meat shelves, with high end steaks being the crowd favorite. Choice of potato,vegetable and beverage. At this time, it became legal to sell Coors beer on this side of the Rockies. This too became a crowd favorite among the boys Big raise, good food,and friends. The stuff summers were made for. By 7am, our shift ended.A new ritual was born. We would all pile into Crazy Johnny's decrepit van and travel almost an hour to the beach. We would sleep most of the day on the sand and under towels. The choice of transportation could have been a factor into the sleepy condition we all experienced. The van had a problem with the heat and defrost being stuck on High. The temperature in the van was inhumane. Another decision which should have had more thought put into it was tackling the off road trails at the beach. The van was not equipped to handle the rigors of off-roading and bogged down in the sand 5 miles from our campsite. No help in sight, we set off in the summer heat hoping to stay alive along the way back. As we returned, we noticed a group of workers from the store waiting for us. They had heard of our plan and decided to meet up with us. It is important to mention that this group, mainly female, were not associated with the girlfriends. We spent most of the summer meeting these, and different groups of girls, almost every day. We would leave for home with enough time to shower and get back to work.The only drawback to life at the beach was giving up the Friday nights out with the boys. Hey, it was only for the summer. As the summer fun continued, CPA Mike decided to go body surfing. He returned to his blanket bleeding from head to toe from being dragged across the broken shells at the waterline. He didn't even realize he was hurt until we pointed it out. He headed for the lifeguard station for repairs. While looking for a clean towel to hand him, we noticed that the one young lady joining us for the day was asleep. She was wearing a white bikini which would have been fine if it wasn't "that time of the month". She awoke horrified and embarrassed and ran to the waves. As she returned, she was in the same condition as Mike, bleeding and crying. The two of them headed to the lifeguards. We decided to leave this situation alone. Our little secret. Due to the fact that we ended up doing a good job with the summer position, our stock began to rise. In the fall, some of the crew were asked to become temporary field help working with struggling stores. They would spend a week or two helping grocery departments, in sister stores, get back into shape. I was asked to help with remodels which eventually led to helping stores close. Not my fault. The company was downsizing and eliminating underperforming stores. We didn't get involved with the politics, we just wanted to keep full time.

Chapter 11-Free For All...Literally

As more stores began to close, the future didn't seem so bright. I went back to my original store as a grocery manager. A promotion at the bitter end. As luck would have it, most of the crew had their futures planned.Losing this job did not mean the end for them. Sadly, I was waiting to be a victim. No plans. Just roll with it. As a store would close, the remaining stock was up for grabs.I remember emptying an entire cigarette cabinet and after loading my car with cartons, only had a sliver of windshield to see out of as I drove home. The supervisor in charge of these closing stores was a stereotypical Irishman. He was clueless and actually pointed out the worthwhile things to take. I ended up with a professional set of butcher knives, 4 foot cutting boards, and assorted office furniture. We later found out that the owners of the company left for South America with all the company's money. Most of the supervision remained on the job in hopes of resurrecting the business. My store manager left for the main office and was running things for a little while. With no deliveries coming in, it was only a matter of time. He set up shop in the central warehouse and was constantly calling us there to help. We arranged deliveries with some of the suppliers who were willing to take the chance along with us. We would answer phones but mostly provided emotional support. The boss was busy making deals he could benefit from. He loved his beer and had closed door meetings with many of the beer suppliers.Reality set in when he asked a few of us to drive to his house in a rented van.The van was loaded with every type of beer on the market.When we got to his house, he met us in the driveway waving a garage door opener in the air. When the door opened, we were amazed to see the entire garage arranged by signs hanging on the wall designating where the cases of beer should be stacked. Not a lawnmower, tool, or car part could be found in that garage. You could have eaten off the floor. This man was passionate.

Needless to say, but the boss used his position for personal gains and the business fell.

Chapter 12-Moving On

My recent promotion looked good on an application so I used it to my advantage. I applied to and was hired by a rival supermarket closer to home. I started attending college as this seemed the way to go. I was not banking on staying with this company after graduating. College was a last minute decision and it resulted in me being the oldest freshman in the program. I wanted to expand my artistic abilities and ended up with an Advertising Art and Design curriculum. It was not what I had envisioned for my talent to be brought to greater heights. I learned all about layouts, paste-ups, and the horrible lessons in drafting. Drafting was a college term for math, which I always hated.

I had worked to save some money to put towards tuition as my High School grades were not good enough to score me a scholarship. I also did not qualify for any type of financial aid so I worked full time nights and full time student days. I paid my way through 3 years of college by working an additional part time job at an actual ad agency. So now I'm working full time at the store,part time at the agency, and on the weekends ran a route involving driving up and down the town deodorizing diner and restaurant bathrooms. Very glamorous! I was exhausted but determined to keep up with my friends who all followed their dreams and finished school. Determination led me to Grandma who was coerced into paying for semester number 4. I graduated , despite drafting, in two years and landed a job in my chosen, but not favorite, field. Entry level with entry level pay. Surprise! No one explained this tidbit of information was the reality of starting a real job. So now I was working full time at another agency and part time at the store. The store was still paying me four times the money I was earning as an artist. Even at part time! The path was laid out before me. Must have been my college education kicking in. Goodbye art. Goodbye dreams. Goodbye to ever paying Grandma back. Hello supermarket, my old friend. The new company took me on as a full time dairy clerk. I've been here before.

This was one of the busiest stores in a chain of over 100 stores spanning the whole of Long Island and parts of upstate New York. It was a family owned company catering mostly to a kosher clientele, if you get my drift. The unfortunate part was that I entered this alone. No crew.No history. The job was demanding due to the amount of dairy that we sold. After a while, a position opened up. Backroom Marker. This position was comprised of unloading trucks and separating them by aisles,similar to my last company. Every case needed to be opened, priced the items inside, and closed the case. We would process fifteen hundred of these cases a day,every day. I was working with an experienced marker. Clay seemed like a normal, level headed guy. He was patient and never raised his voice. He was focused on getting the work done in the time allotted and leaving on time.I was beginning to get that "9 year speed' after all. Damn! I enjoyed this position as you were able to wear shorts and listen to music as loudly as you wanted to. Together, we were able to process the trucks with ease. A little backroom organization, a quick sweep, and the day was over for us. As much as Clay was organized, he was certifiable. He was an ex-con who started working here after his parole. His true colors shone when one of the soda vendors took a cart without asking. Clay was planning to use the cart and in a calm voice asked the man not to use it. He needed it. The vendor ignored him and stood on the loading dock as his truck was backing in. Clay walked over to him and punched him in the face with such force it knocked the man off the dock. Clay calmly took the cart back to our area and simply went back to work. Clay's antics finally caught up to him the day a case of glass bottled apple juice fell from the pallet we were unloading, hitting him in the head. He laid on the loading dock, unconscious, which felt like forever. He was taken to the hospital and we never heard from him again.He was replaced with another marker from a busy store, Petey. Petey kept an actual samurai sword tucked neatly away at his workstation. I never saw him use it, but I heard the stories. I had heard there was a frozen food manager position available in a neighboring store. I saw this as my opportunity to escape the crazies that worked the backrooms.

Chapter 13- Mickey(God Help Us All)

After accepting the position, my career took many turns. I was transferred three times in three years. These were all positive moves based on my reputation for running a good department. Further proof of my capabilities was being asked to set up frozen departments in some of the drawing board stores. This company was growing and opening at least one new store a year. I would arrive to write the initial orders and assist in product placement. I worked side by side with a number of frozen food supervisors. One of these stores had an overwhelming frozen food department. It consisted of two 80 foot aisles containing 36 doors on each side. Down the middle of this oversized aisle were two 80 foot long open well cases. These were where you would shop for frozen vegetables,cans of juice, and a full variety of ice cream. The doors held dinners, cakes , international brands and the like. It was always the same department specialists showing up for the new store set ups. I had to help with dairy and worked with the same specialist for the last two openings. Mickey was a younger guy who could have been mistaken for Rick Springfield. He received a lot of attention from the young ladies. He literally had his hands full for most of the day, if you get my meaning. Hewas approached by many of the newly hired cashier trainees offering him anything from food to sex. Things did not change much for him once the store opened for business. The cashier's attention were replaced with the female shoppers taking over. He and I were working in the same aisle on one particular day. A strange couple were shopping in the aisle and walked up to us with a question. We had seen them shopping in the store before today. The husband was obviously handicapped as he struggled to keep up to his wife. She appeared to be much younger and very attractive. The husband staggered over to us and made us a financial offer to come home with them and have sex with his wife. He was only going to watch as he was unable to satisfy her any longer. I became terrified feeling there was an underlying plan involving the husband . Did he want to film this or somehow get involved with all three of us? Mickey was excited about this proposition and was practically begging me to go through with it. I kept imagining the husband in the background . Drooling and sweating. There was no way I was taking part in any of this nightmare situation. To this day, I still feel nauseous reliving this story. "If you change your mind, let me know"' Oh hell no! After opening these two stores, Mickey and I went our separate ways. In a way I was relieved to be rid of him and his obsession with women. I remained there as the frozen food manager as he moved onto a smaller store as a general manager. Our paths would cross again in a few years.

Chapter 14-Bobby C

I had nothing but respect for my current store manager. He ended up to be my role model and still is to this day. He could criticize,threaten,and belittle you and after he was done ranting, stopped to buy both of us coffee and hang out for thirty minutes as friends. An amazing man but far from amazing returning after his day off. That day, once a week on a Thursday,nothing was right, nobody did any work on Wednesday and on and on for the first few hours in the morning. Stay away until lunch. He would encourage me to use my artistic talent to benefit the store.After he saw me winning merchandising contests in frozen food, he approached me with different projects around the store. One example was turning the entire cashier area into a western town to promote a meat contest. The front wall of the store, behind the registers, was a series of doors and the customer service desk. This was transformed into a jail, saloon,sheriff's office,and church using painted cardboard and broken wooden boards from the backroom. We also supported a seafood promotion by rigging a huge net from the ceiling above the department. The greatest encouragement from him was what I called , the morale booster. He had me create caricatures of all the employees in the store. These were done on poster board and were hung on the backroom wall. There were over 100 employees so this took some time. I'll never forget pulling in for work and seeing him on the sidewalk waiting for me."How many did you bring?" he asked, expecting me to have more drawings. When I told him I couldn't get anything done the night before, he sent me home to come back with at least one.

Chapter 15-Eddie

My only obstacle in the way of having fun at work was the District Manager.This man was in charge of fifteen stores that made up one district. We didn't see eye to eye would be a big understatement. He was an arrogant, ex-military man with a bald head and a Wyatt Earp mustache to go with it. I never understood what he had against me as he transferred me from store to store in hopes I would quit. I stuck it out which I'm sure frustrated the hell out of him. Maybe it was the curse of being born with flaming red hair that put everyone on the defensive towards me. I stood out and was always the person they noticed and watched.Enough with the paranoia. During this latest opening, I was in the stockroom throwing out my cardboard and trash. Cardboard was put into a crushing machine which turned out enormous cubes of flattened boxes that a third party would ship to Japan. There was a lot of money involved in the selling of these bales. Straight up trash was thrown into an opening in the wall which led to a container. I was running from machine to machine as one flattened and the other was compacting trash. Being in a hurry, while standing at the baler, I noticed a bag of peas I had neglected to place in the trash. I assume, out of frustration,I threw the bag in the direction of the chute. My aim was off as the bag hit the wall and spewed frozen peas all over the backroom floor. Just at that moment, the DM entered the area and witnessed this with great disappointment. He calmly asked "What do you call that?". I calmly answered "A miss...Eddie". He didn't find this as funny as the rest of the crew lining up for trash did. This move added to my resume. My only savior in many of these situations was my manager Bobby C. He had a long relationship with Eddie and always managed to smooth over my screw ups with him. During another opening, as I reported for my first day in a store that was still under construction, I noticed Eddie was the only one there as I always arrived early. He didn't see me come in because of the dimly lit conditions and I observed him doing some inspection on the construction. I had about 30 minutes before I officially reported for work and decided to keep a low profile until others started arriving. I crawled into a register stand and remained out of sight. The Assistant Manager, appointed to this store ,was down one of the dimly lit aisles trying to place an order.He needed to write the number of cases needed and was getting frustrated because he couldn't see what he was doing. Eddie decided to see what he was yelling about and as he approached was greeted with "Leave me the hell alone Eddie, I'm not in the mood!" This opened a very loud dialogue between the two men as I crawled further into my stand. I couldn't believe how this manager was getting away with speaking to him this way. After much back and forth, Eddie decided it would be in his best interest to leave him alone. Bravo! This man was obviously under a lot of pressure. I had a relatively easy day after that. Years later, at a wedding of co-workers, I was seated at the same table with Bobby and yes,Eddie and his wife. Eddie had been drinking and when he saw me sit down next to him, threw his arm around me." I always liked you John". I sipped my drink and without lifting my head replied "You are so full of shit Eddie, you never liked me".His wife was laughing so hard her drink was coming out of her nose and she ended up spewing all over Eddie's suit, Karma at last!

Chapter 16- Oh Jimmy

After Eddie retired, I got to work with another gem of a man. This DM made Eddie look like a Boy Scout. I always assumed he told Eddie he would carry the torch that would get me to leave. The ridiculous part of this relationship was that Jimmy, the new DM, was best friends with Mickey's brother. They grew up together and worked together at this company for many years. This did not help me. It is NOT who you know! At this point in my career I was now an Assistant Manager. This was a coveted position as you were still a union member and had some protection. Jimmy was a lot younger than Eddie so our relationship would become a long one. I continued to be the focus of attention. I was constantly questioned and challenged. During one of these challenges, Jimmy called me a liar. I quickly responded "You only lie to people you fear and you don't scare me!". I won the day but there were many more battles to win. As I was challenged on my closing procedures, I have to say he was right on this one. We were required to secure the roll-up doors in the backroom before we left for the evening. I forgot, more than once, to roll these doors down. It was easy to forget when you are dealing with money, shopping carts, departments, and alarms. One evening, I got a heads up that Jimmy was in the store. I immediately raced to the stockroom to secure the once again open doors. Rather than use the chain and pulley system to lower the first door, I decided to jump up and grab the bottom of the door to pull it down. This would be faster. I jumped up but didn't come down. I was hanging by my index finger which was impaled on an exposed rivet securing the weather stripping. I remained swinging from the finger until the skin ripped and set me free. I immediately went to the meat department. The butchers were the store's surgical team as they had to deal with all kinds of bloody atrocities. If ever someone got cut, they promptly headed to meat. The meat manager sat me down and began to bandage my hand to stop the bleeding. I loosened my tie and did my best to keep from fainting. Jimmy walked in, saw me in the chair with my hand bandaged to the wrist, and out of concern for my welfare said "you are out of uniform". Thanks Jim! After closing the store, in full uniform god knows, I went to the emergency room and received 8 stitches butI kept my tie on!

Chapter 17- Bending The Rules

Closing the store was always an issue. You are tired. You have a million responsibilities to adhere to. The store was slated to close at 10pm. It was clearly posted on the doors. It would be obvious to normal people that having the departments shut off their lights as they left would be a sign we were ready to leave. Most of our customers were not ready to leave with us. We made announcements concerning closing. We would threaten that the registers would shut down at 10pm. The most effective ploy, for me, when noticing there were many shoppers left in the store at 945, lock the IN door stopping more imbeciles from coming in. Doing the math, the remaining shoppers should hopefully be rung up and out by 10. Great idea until the one night Jimmy decided to visit us at 945.The entrance door and exit door were separated by a half wall. Jimmy pulled his company car right up to the EXIT door. He pulled the door open and came in. He never realized the IN door was locked for the past fifteen minutes. Dodging a bullet here is the understatement of the century. The second greatest deviation in closing was making an announcement concerning security. With the loveless shoppers in no hurry to leave, we would announce "Okay Bob, everyone is out...release the dogs!" Oh my God! All you heard was the panic stricken lollygaggers all racing up to the registers. My personal favorite. Another time, a customer came into the store the same way Jimmy did. An elderly Asian man was walking towards me. "I'm sorry,we're closed". He pretended not to understand English and mumbled something as he pushed past me. "I can't wait to hear the reason you give the police for trespassing in a closed store". He stopped dead in his tracks,turned around and went out the door.Another win! I had a closing cashier with a DJ voice take care of the announcements. One of the grocery workers was back from vacation after getting married. This poor soul was the brunt of much bullying as he worked full time as a postal worker. He was sickly thin and his bride was at least four times bigger than him. What would you expect from the rest of the crew with this kind of ammunition? During the nightly closing announcements, the DJ, not realizing there were still shoppers in the store, made an historic announcement congratulating him and his bride on his wedding. When he added that the honeymoon video was on sale at the customer service counter put it over the top. Just when we thought it was over," Watch Jeff slap her belly and ride the wave in!" Still one of the funniest moments in my life. All done in that DJ voice which I can STILL hear! Thanks for the memories!

Chapter 18-Round 2

After being transferred 40 miles from home, I still couldn't shake Jimmy. Upon arriving here for my first day, I met my new manager, Mickey. Here we go again. First thing out of his mouth was a list of cashiers and other assorted females that I should stay away from as he had claimed them all to be his. We walked upstairs to the office which overlooked much of the cashier area. In the middle of filling me in about the store, he looked at the window and said to me"Watch this". There was a twenty something shopper getting on line to checkout. MIckey keyed the microphone that was part of the overhead public address system."Hi honey! Up here! How you doing today?"' The young woman looked up at us and promptly gave Mickey the finger. She started to load her purchases on the belt, still ignoring the men in the window. Mickey was unrelenting."What's wrong honey? On the rag?" Really. On the rag. The entire store heard this and was in disbelief but this was Mickey.Ladies Man to the end. Between this reckless behavior, and many sexual harassment suits filed against him, family friend or not, Jimmy was forced to terminate him. The Vice President of the company arrived the next day to introduce us to our new Store Manager. This man's entire experience was based in the meat department of a rival market but was friends with the VP. He would work out just fine. Paul was a little older than retirement age. A man that took no chances showing up in suspenders and a belt. After the introductions were over, the VP leaned over to me and asked me to show Paul the ropes. Oh what? I'm not qualified enough to have his job but qualified enough to be his teacher. A few days later we began to see a pattern with Paul. He would come down from his office every afternoon at 3pm wanting to walk the backroom and comment on conditions. The grocery manager and myself would walk with this man as he named all the groceries his wife, Violet, would buy."Redpack tomatoes...Violet uses these. Coca Cola...Violet buys those". This seemed to go on forever. The grocery manager, who never found fault in anyone, turned to me during this latest walk and uttered the most epic line I have ever heard."We have ourselves a real knowledgeable motherfucker right here!" Thanks Kevin! I attempted to explain the receiving process for accepting deliveries to the store to Paul. The deliveries would come through the back door so as not to be in the way of the shoppers. This was an important part of the bookkeeping of the store. Paul assured me he understood the process. The next morning, I arrived after Paul who had taken a bar stool from one of the offices and set up a receiving station at the customer service desk in the front of the store. The line of vendors and products stretched into the vestibule, a good 200 feet from the desk. The DM walked in and upon seeing this asked me what he was doing. "Receiving Jimmy! He assured me he had it!". You could train a puppy easier than an ex butcher. Another argument with JImmy ensued but this time was overheard by the dairy manager. Hermy was an intimidating Spanish man standing at 6 foot 3 and weighing in around 300 pounds. He had no respect for authority but would do his job. After Jimmy walked away, Hermy motioned me to come into his aisle. He looked in either direction as he made this proposal."I have some friends who would take that guy to the Bronx in the back of a van, strip him naked,paint him pink,and leave him there for dead"'.All of this could be arranged by tonight. I quickly thanked him for looking out for me but assured him that it wouldn't be necessary. Not right now anyway! Hermy was like the big, insane older brother. The owners loved him. Maybe they heard the "pink" story?

Chapter 19-Bobbing And Weaving

Thank god I was needed in yet another new store opening in the eastern part of Long Island. I was getting closer to home finally. I was sent to continue my role as an Assistant Manager. The store was enormous and actually needed an assistant to oversee multiple departments. I was one of five in charge of dairy and frozen, my forte. It seemed obvious to me that this store manager was under orders to continue making my life miserable. I was able to roll with whatever he dished out. Amateur! Whenever he was due to leave for the day, he would walk the store with that particular assistant that would be closing.He would leave them with obvious tasks to ensure a clean and smooth closing. We referred to this as "walking the dog". One night, when I was closing, he began his walk with me. To refer to my list of tasks as a laundry list would be understating it. This was a ridiculous amount of work to complete by closing, but I let him talk.

Halfway around the back of the store, I heard him gasp and grab his chest. He fell to one knee still holding his chest. I glanced back over my shoulder and continued to walk and scribble notes. As he started to feel better, he caught up to me and asked"Didn't you see me go down back there"? I replied "Yes, but I thought you spotted a quarter on the floor". Needless to say I was very disappointed that he actually got up. He continued to try and get the better of me up until Thanksgiving week. He called me into his office to tell me the produce manager was out on workmans compensation and would be out till after the holiday. I would need to run the produce department until he returned. I knew absolutely nothing about produce but what the hell. Long story short, Best week of produce sales in the history of the store. I had a blast writing massive orders and building massive displays out of them. The produce crew came to the party and did whatever needed to be done. I was now able to stick this assignment up the store manager's ass! Happy Thanksgiving shithead!

Chapter 20-My Artwork Takes Center Stage

Hoping for a way out, the produce supervisor, noticing the job I had done over the holiday, offered me a new position. Thankfully this position was not to bury me in some troubled produce store but to use my art. It was called The Farmstand Project. All the department signage was removed and replaced with hanging chalkboards. It was my job to travel from store to store and using pastels, create new hand drawn signs. Each sign also needed to include a hand drawn picture of whatever fruit or vegetable was being advertised. Sounds cushy but with 96 stores each having 40 boards, this translated into a lot of work.The rules were simple.Travel to the designated store,finish the boards front and back, and oh yeah, do not work any overtime. I was also told to interview creative people in the store to see who could maintain the signs week to week. The company suggested that I should train people in my style,but this never happened. At first, everything went according to plan. I would submit an expense report and get reimbursed for gas. I traveled to stores near my home as they were converted from east to west. The deeper I got, the worse it got to be. I was traveling 100 miles a day. Brooklyn, the Bronx, remote areas of upstate New York. I was paying tolls and racking up many miles on my car. I also had to go out of order if one store had a visit from supervision requiring immediate changes. 96 stores. Not one talented person to be found. I was doubling back to certain stores weekly when the prices changed. This went on for 2 years. I thought I was a rock star but came to find out the company took all my art and had it reproduced as magnets. No permission. No commission. Typical.By the way, the gas money was short lived as well. The one highlight I can remember was borrowing my wife's brand new Mitsubishi Spyder. I needed to go to Brooklyn on this day and thought I would give my car a rest. I entered the store and was forced to work on their boards in the backroom due to lack of space on the sales floor. I spent my 8 hours completing the boards and upon leaving was met with 6 inches of snow that had fallen throughout the day. The problem was the car was only 4 inches off the ground and had a six speed manual shift. Long story short, 4 hour trip, bumper to bumper, brand new car,stick shift,do the math! The dream job ended after two full years of touring New York and I was placed back into the stores.

Chapter 21-Racism

The first morning back into the stores, I was asked to be the opener. This store ran an overnight stocking crew that was managed by a veteran Night Manager, Bob. Bob was an older African American man dressed in a sort of tactical style. He was simple yet organized and ran a good crew. This particular morning, as I arrived, I witnessed Bob standing in the doorway awaiting my arrival. This would be his cue to go home. Bob was joined by the night porter. He was an older man of Spanish descent. Bob had asked him to clean in and around the front door area. The porter took offense to a Black man giving him orders."Do you think you are better than me? I do not work for you." This being said, he promptly loosened his pants, turned around and aimed his naked rear at Bob. "Why don't you kiss my ass!" As the argument escalated, who should come into the store, at the scene of the argument, Jimmy the D.M. I left him to clean this up as I had a job to do. Just another day in a series of good days in this paradise.

Chapter 22-Mikey The Legend

Mornings seemed to be the setting for how the rest of the day was going to shape up. Summertime. Our small and pot-holed ridden parking lot became the stage for police cars, SWAT teams, and reporters. A drug store, located in the corner of our strip mall was being robbed by thieves armed with automatic weapons. Upon seeing the police, they started shooting up the store in an attempt to escape. Our store remained closed for most of the day. The grocery manager and I left to play handball at the beach. An opportunity for an Assistant Manager became available so I agreed to head out east once again. It was hard to leave some of these people as we became lifelong friends. My newly appointed store was a low volume, older building relying on a customer base of nursing home patients. There was a path, through a field,that went from the home to our store. The Store Manager was brand new and a friend of mine. This could work out to be beneficial. Once again, a qualified team of workers trying to succeed, with the odds of success against them. Without being able to increase the business, we would be scrutinized for payroll, over ordering, and never doing enough to please

the powers that be. One payroll obstacle was Mikey. Mikey was our porter slash wagon boy. Mikey was in the union for many years and was making one of the top salaries in the store. Mikey was a five foot tall, mentally disabled,older man who must have failed hygiene in school. He had dental benefits but chose to survive with his three remaining teeth. He had an enormous belly which was constantly in view as he would allow his t-shirt to ride up on it. Throughout his extensive stay with the company, he was rarely transferred due to having no transportation and his huge salary. He was constantly teased and would use what was said to him to retaliate. His biggest catch phrase, that he picked up from some of the part timers, was "Ya Mudda" followed by a long, loud sigh. I can still hear this. When Mikey was hot...sigh. When Mikey was tired...sigh. When Mikey was asked to do ANYTHING...sigh. The sighs were always followed by his toothless grin and a belly rub to top it off. After being asked to collect carts, Mikey tried to resist by blaming the heat. Refusing to let him avoid doing his job, I insisted he do his job and forced him outside. The shirt came up, the sighs began but now he would approach the customers to tell them "John Calada, he hates me, he wants me dead!" Just perfect. Here I am defending myself against Mikey and the people that love him. Another facet of his tasks was emptying and sorting the recycled bottles and cans. These were stored in plastic bags in a corner of the stockroom. As time went on, the smell from this corner became more offensive. At first we all assumed it was stale beer, but as the days dragged on it became clear that it was, in fact, urine! As the union representative, Gene, was walking the store, we asked him to help us in speaking with Mikey about the corner. No accusations, just asking. Gene could be more diplomatic in a situation like this and it would also keep us out of trouble for blaming anyone. Gene agreed and asked Mikey to come with him to the back where the store manager and I were waiting. As Gene began to explain right and wrong , Mikey became very nervous. He looked at us, looked around the room, seeming to avoid answering any questions until asked "Do you understand what I'm saying?". Mikey fired back "YES, SOMEBODY'S PISSIN...IT AINT ME! And Gene (wait for it) YA MUDDA EATS IT!" You know, what you would say to the man who protects your job.

Chapter 23- There's A Lot Going On

In keeping with the bodily fluid theme, upon entering the stockroom of one of my many appointed stores, I was greeted with a surprise. The stockroom is generally considered off limits to the shopping public so you can imagine my confusion seeing two men standing with their backs to me in the backroom. The one man was helping his eighty year old father urinate onto a pallet of cat litter. All he said was"He had to go". I immediately asked him if he was raised in a barn because this is where we sell food, " I thought the cat litter would absorb it" was his only defense. "Generally, you would be correct" I replied, being one second away from losing my mind. The cat litter would work better if it was already opened". My next brush with ecoli came from an elderly woman asking to use the ladies room. After giving her foolproof directions, including climbing an immense staircase leading to the upstairs facilities, she thanked me and proceeded. Later I learned that she apparently made it halfway up leaving me a surprise along the way. During a particularly busy day, while the bulk of the workers were making their way outside to view an overturned car, I was approached again. A different elderly woman with the same request. At this time there was an alternate restroom located at the end of a backroom hallway. Granted it was a little hard to find. One wrong turn brought you to a dead end of refrigerated storage doors. This is where she ended up. As I went to check on an item located inside one of those freezers, I walked up on the woman wrestling her dress off her head. Her panties were down and she continued relieving herself unaware I was there. When the dress was lifted off, she embarrassingly tried to get dressed and apologized profusely. My only horror filled question "Who is cleaning this mess off my floor"? She swore she would take care of it and grabbed a meat apron to smear the pile. She left me feeling she had helped and all would be forgiven except for the fact of tossing the apron onto a stack of clean uniforms. Between this and the car accident, so much to see in so little time.

Chapter 24-Tommy...Yeah!

Tommy was a transplant from Brooklyn. He was a cross between Elvis and Fonzie. A total stereotype. Tommy was a good worker but more than a handful to control. You just could not get the Brooklyn out of the boy. It was a few days before Passover and being a Kosher market,we had a reputation for carrying many different types of holiday foods. A rabbi was shopping the aisles when he approached Tommy." Excuse me. Can you direct me to your challah bread?" Tommy, knowing the stock, politely told the rabbi we had sold out but were expecting another delivery tomorrow. This was not what the man wanted to hear." What do you mean...sold out. How is that possible? It's the holidays. You people run a kosher store for god's sake". This man was enraged. Tommy sprang into action. He threw an arm around the rabbi and hugged him. He then uttered the most memorable statement I have heard up until this point in my career." Hey...calm down Moe. Youre gonna give yourself a fuckin heart attack over some fuckin bread." This is what you say to an irate man of the cloth. I'm surprised he didn't have a fuckin heart attack because of what Tommy said. Tommy would take his lunch break everyday at 3pm. This seemed a little late to me to be taking lunch but I assumed he had a reason. He did. The bank next door would close at three and the young tellers would all leave together to go home. Tommy sat on a kiddie ride smoking a cigarette. "Hey honey...over here...wanna take a ride on my horsey?". When a contingent of bank tellers stormed the store to speak to the manager, I could not have been less surprised. "Is it possible to keep The Lone Ranger inside of the store until we get into our cars?" Tommy...come to the office!

Chapter 25-Taking My Best Shot

Along the same lines as Mikey, there was Bobby. Bobby had Down's Syndrome but was very dedicated to his job as a porter slash wagon boy. Bobby was also with the union for a long period of time. One of his favorite benefits was that he qualified for a four week vacation based on his years on the job. Bobby would invest his pay into buying and renting apartment buildings which funded his vacations. When I first met him, as he was explaining all this to me, he also stated that he has seen half the world already and would not stop until he sees the rest. All i could say was "Bobby...you're not retarded...I AM!" The store that he was assigned to was run by the most evil of all the managers. He would abuse Bobby by sending him out in the rain to collect wagons from the middle of puddles. As karma would have it, this manager had some sort of breakdown and was found crying in the backroom behind the baler. Whatever problem he had, he never returned to work. I was able to keep tabs on him as he was my cousin's next door neighbor. I'm sure Bobby will be thinking about you as he sails by icebergs in Alaska. Loser! I began to be asked to step in and help out as a temporary store manager in a few locations. These stores were either in the stages of being remodeled or closing. My first appointment was in a larger store that had been having departments closed down due to poor sales. There was a boarded up seafood department and plans to do the same to the bakery. The bakery manager was moved to another location leaving a full time employee in charge of the failing department. Nice lady. She was doing her best under these conditions when Thanksgiving was approaching. She came to me and explained that she had run out of pumpkin pies. The store would make them from scratch but she ran out of ingredients. In a classic managerial move, I noticed the frozen food freezer was floor to ceiling high with leftover Mrs. Smith's pies from last year. I transferred these pies to the bakery and with the help of the grocery boys, was able to produce and package enough pies to get us through the holiday. At my weekly department manager meeting, I would ask for suggestions to try and increase the business in this failing store. One of the better suggestions was to take the day-old bagels, cut them into chips, and arrange them on a platter with a small cup of salsa in the middle. This idea went from garbage to a $6.99 sale! Genius. This discussion became very popular with my crew. The ideas were working as I encouraged every scheme they could come up with. The sales may have improved but the plan for shrinking the store still existed. I remained in this store until a newly hired store manager, with ties to the CEO ,was hired. He lived down the street from the store and the idea of not having to commute to work suited him. I moved on to the next disaster and immediately formed a hatred for my replacement.

Chapter 26-Eighteen Years And Counting

By now I am sure most of you are asking" Damn...how many stores did this guy work in?". As of my latest 'promotion' I have already invested 17 years of my life with this company. I was asked to go back to Mikey's store as acting, but not getting the pay, manager. The company was planning to start remodeling so I was asked to babysit as we ran down the stock. This may be where my nickname began. I was now known as The Grim Reaper. If I showed up at your store, it was destined to close. Short term or forever but the writing was on the wall for change. I progressed to a three man crew as we would travel the island to supervise the closings, The company was streamlining and investing in larger stores with larger sales volumes. Myself and my crew would be on standby when a decision concerning a specific store arose. In the meantime, yes,I was assigned to another store as a co-manager. Worst job in the company by far. You were not the manager and you shared none of the responsibilities. The only advantage in making co-managers was the fact they were taken out of the union and placed on salary. Oh boy...more free hours I get to work The stores were not the only thing getting streamlined. The corporate office jobs, located inside the massive warehouse, were also being dissolved.Secretaries, warehouse workers,and other non-essential workers were losing their positions. The store I was sent to had the honor of saving one of the secretaries jobs. Her husband was a store manager and the VP she worked for had this great idea in making her a manager. No experience whatsoever! None! This is when I heard a familiar phrase from the VP" Teach her everything you know!".AGAIN? My decision was made at this point. If I'm not good enough to have her job, I'm out of here. I was not irrational enough to leave without having somewhere to go. It would just be a matter of time. That time came sooner than I expected.

Chapter 27-Frequent-Flyer Y'all

After posting my resume, I assumed it would be an endless wait for anyone to react to it. I had almost 20 years of experience starting with full time grocery to the dizzying heights of store manager. While waiting almost two weeks, I received a voicemail from a grocery headhunter. We started negotiating for a position in South Carolina for a Supermarket Store Manager. Holy crap! Lots of things to consider. The recruiter arranged a meeting including 3 flights to Charleston. I was met by a town car. The driver held up the little sign with my name on it. Rock star! I met with the Human Resource Director and had a long, detailed chat with him. This was the second interview of my life. I had no idea what was expected of me. It must have went well as he had me back for a follow up to do some paperwork. I also traveled back to meet him for a typical store tour. Three flights! Pretty cool! Alas, after some thought, I politely declined the position. I had received another offer from the same recruiter and wanted to explore my options. This job was located in North Carolina. Another flight and another interview. My third! I think back and foolishly spoke about the offer in SC. This must have put pressure on Fred, the Human Resource Manager. He offered me the same salary I was making in New York and explained I would be involved in a 3 month training program. They would arrange lodging and an expense account for meals. The training started in July which gave me time to give my notice and get my life in order. I accepted the position, after considering my family's feelings. I needed to sell my house and arrange for movers. I decided to drive one of our cars to the hotel they provided for me and arrived on Sunday. Monday starts the training program. Monday morning consisted of paperwork and meeting the other 14 newly hired Store Manager Trainees. Some of these men were locals. Most of us came from other states. At this time, no one had bothered to explain that this company was also in trouble. In their long history, they had never hired from the outside. They would always promote from within. This explains the fat salaries and living accommodations as they had no idea of what they were doing. The training was amazing and would stay with me for the rest of my career. As a trainee, you were required to work alongside the respective department supervisor. These supervisors were responsible for 12 stores. When working with the Meat supervisor, I would spend two weeks traveling store to store as he made his rounds. I was taught everything from grinding chop meat to cleaning the department at the end of the day. After the second week, I was followed with a clipboard and asked to perform many functions in the department. Their philosophy was that if no one was in the department to help a customer, you could step in and do anything they needed to avoid losing a sale. New York should have thought like this! I fried chicken and sliced cold cuts in the deli. I had to physically make a wedding cake in the bakery. I knew how to properly prepare catfish in seafood. Of course, you learned bookkeeping and running a register but it made sense to know these things. I aced the clipboard test and was assigned a store located on the outskirts of Raleigh. I was met by the District Manager who introduced me to the crew.

Chapter 28-Meet John From New York, Rednecks

From the outset, these people were not thrilled to be working for a Yankee Especially a New York Yankee.Something I never considered.The meat manager took the most exception to me. He was uncooperative and nasty. After asking him to help with a specific meat issue, his attitude drove me to finally saying " That's it. We need to take this out back and I can assure you that only one of us is coming back inside!" He immediately backed down promising me things would be different going forward. I couldn't let it go as I was still pumped." You lost the war 138 years ago, get past it already!" Things improved between him and I. The customer service girl found my accent to be very amusing. Like hers wasn't? Illiterate! She approached me, followed by two friends that had come to the store. In a giddy voice she asked me to say something. As I tried to ignore her, she kept asking me to say something, anything. I finally gave in, leaned over to her and said "You are fired...get out!" Still funny! Things slowly improved at the store once the employees realized I was for real. I was fair but still got tested. The few that I managed to win over were very helpful in making all this work. The manager that I replaced was an alcoholic and lost his job. I fully understand. I used basic merchandising techniques to change some things and the crew respondedI After All, I did bring some big city experience to Mayberry. Not unlike New York, I still had to deal with the homeless and people begging for money on the sidewalk. A delivery of 50 gas grills arrived at the store. I was directed to display them on the sidewalk in front of the store. One tiny problem, they all needed to be assembled. After exploring all my options, I asked the street people if they would be interested in a free lunch. They got busy and by the time the sun was setting, completed all fifty. Two men. Two sandwiches. Being that it was also 90 degrees that day, two bottles of water, This move still haunts me but they were very appreciative. With another day coming to an end, it was time to head back to my 2 bedroom condo that I negotiated with Fred. I explained that my house in New York was still not sold and my wife and kids were coming to stay with me. The hotel would no longer work for us. This condo was on a lake. You could fish and go canoeing. There was a lighted tennis court and an indoor pool. Why go to work?

Still capitalizing on the fact that he had no idea what he was doing, we remained here until finally buying a house in a nearby town. The house was built on spec and was never occupied until we purchased it. The house was a beautiful Victorian style which we could never afford back home. Property tax was almost non-existent. I was able to buy a brand new pick-up and furnish the house from front to back. New York money goes a long way down south. The only negatives were pizza and Chinese food! But seriously, we were 45 minutes away from civilization as our house was part of a developed tobacco farm. With two kids to keep occupied, my wife had her fill of Carolina but suffered through for my benefit. Upon being hired, it would have been beneficial to know that we were all part of an experiment. They had flirted with the idea of eliminating all the stores they owned from Maryland to Florida. In a last ditch effort, they hired outside help in hopes of saving these stores. The decision was made one year after we all started our employment. They decided to close the east coast stores remaining in Texas and points south. As unemployment benefits do not exist in Carolina, we had no choice but to sell our home and move back to New York. We ended up breaking even on our house and sold most of our furniture. We rented a box truck and returned to the island. As a last resort, we ended up living with my mom in a Long Island bungalow designed for two, not five.

Chapter 29-Where's My Car?

The hunt for employment began again landing me a position with yet another rival, as an assistant manager. Back to the fast pace of New York. I remained at this position for a short time as I was offered a supervisory position. This chain was growing and growing quickly. In the middle of setting up a new super store, I began to feel homesick for my old kosher company. I began to send out feelers in hopes of returning. After the new store was opened, I remained there as an assistant until the next new store was decided on. This could be months or even years as I was unhappy stepping down to begin with. I heard back from my former employer and was able to return. Once again a co-manager. One step forward etc. Interesting twist, Jimmy the DM moved on to another company since I left and left his wife in charge. She was another of the rescued secretaries from the corporate office. She did a little better not becoming a store manager. She ended up being a pleasure to work with. I had heard that there were interviews for potential store managers. I had friends in Human Resources. I was able to interview with my favorite answer to one question that became legendary. I was working for a weak manager at this time. They asked" What decisions do you help him with on a daily basis?" I stopped before I answered "What should he have for lunch?" I got the position but was disappointed to find out I would be working for a different DM. This man was a trainwreck. It was later determined that at 50 years old, he had Alzheimers. He would forget names and where he parked his car. It was sad because I knew him in the past when he was younger and sharp. I was sent to another in a long line of troubled stores. I know...another store? Yes! This store was being inspected by the new CEO in the upcoming weeks. He was to decide if the company was going to close us or take a chance leaving it open. I assembled the team and we all agreed to put on a show for this man. The displays were impeccable. All the departments were full and inviting. The stock level rose as the backroom stock disappeared. The store team really rose to the occasion. The morning of the visit arrived. The store never looked better. The stakes grew higher as the son of the owner joined the CEO on his walk. I did my best to point out all the potential in the store. The visit seemed to last forever but at the end, the CEO leaned over to me and said ' you have given this store the potential to do five hundred thousand a week. A far cry from the 125 we are used to seeing"'. This was a good day but had no effect on my District Manager. During the next few weeks, seeing what my employees were capable of doing, he started to transfer most of my department managers to troubled stores. Before I knew it, he had stripped mr=e of my most important crew members and placed me in a position to fail. I was not going to let that happen so the hunt for alternate employment became my new goal. I had been in touch with a notable pharmacy chain and was offered a position to manage for them. Without any notice, I turned my store keys into my assistant manager's hand and left. I never looked back! That ends a 27 year run with this company...on and off!

Chapter 30-Dollar Days

In hindsight, the decision to take a drug store job was made in haste. Sure, I was trying to prove a point. The money was good, the most money I have ever made. My benefits were the same benefits as doctors and hospital workers. It was the fact that there were only three aisles of food where I would feel comfortable. As the manager, I would be responsible for allowing the pharmacist to process prescriptions before their due date. A customer would insist that it was a life or death situation and I would agreeably break the law for them. No pressure. Our displays were built on four shelves, three feet high, on the ends of the three aisles. Impressive. We also had a photoshop that required management involvement on a daily basis. I could never understand or get past the' prescription forgiveness 'process and decided this was not for me. I was getting pretty good at quitting jobs, but I always had a back-up plan. The plan was to try my hand at managing a dollar store. I actually stopped the car on the way to the interview to call the DM to tell him I really didn't think this was right for me. He made me feel like I was screwing him by not taking the job which I found complimentary. The interview took place one block from my house, in our local store. There was a sister store one mile further east but I was still very close to home. Beats traveling the island for a place to work. The money was a little less than I was used to but I would save greatly on gas. I started in the local store, did a good enough job to supervise the building of another store in the same neighborhood. I was in charge of hiring. I would hire 100 people to end up with 35. These folks were hand picked.By me! The store opened and proved to be a big success. The district manager liked me. He didn't like many people as a rule. All was good until the day HE was transferred. I would have gone with him but not to Brooklyn. His replacement was a former store manager trying to prove herself at everyones expense. A miserable woman who turned my little world upside down. This may seem hard to believe but I ,once again, read the writing on the wall.

An announcement was made that a rival dollar chain had bought the company I was working for and are planning on merging into one. I made my move. A former employee was working at the new company, also located in the same town. I had spoken to him many times before this day but now I needed a favor. His district manager was about to retire and really didn't care about anything else. When I heard he was in the store, I went to meet with him about jumping sides. My friend couldn't say or do enough for me as he pushed his boss to hire me. One week later, I was in his office,signing paperwork, and wishing him luck on his retirement. I actually gave notice this time, afraid our paths may cross again. Afterall we were both working for the same company. I started, once again, as a store manager. I trained with my friend for two weeks and was turned loose on the dollar spending public.As it turned out, this was a correct decision on my part as the kosher chain closed for good. The dollar store was a lot to deal with. You worked understaffed and had to process large deliveries in the span of two days. Most of my time was spent as a cashier due to the payroll restrictions regarding the hiring of more than one breathing body. The hours were ridiculously long and, being on salary, I was able to earn less than minimum wage as I did the math. A large portion of your day was cleaning up after the bargain hunting morons would tear the store apart. Shoplifting was a regular distraction. If most items cost one dollar then why the hell would you have to steal?! Because of my experience, I started out in the biggest store they had. All the problems of a small store and then some.

This store had a large grocery department as well as dairy and frozen food. The theme of these stores was to open in the lower class neighborhoods. You could not get any lower where I worked. The shoplifting capitol of Long Island. To say that the police would take their breaks in that parking lot would be an understatement. The store was a remodeled pharmacy. The drive up window was boarded shut and a tarp hung on either side. The homeless people who lived in this tent were happy to have it, and their proximity to the store made it easy to steal what they needed. There was a laundromat next door that was owned by a nice Spanish couple. Each day we would say hello and they would frequent my store for detergent and other laundry needs. On one of his shopping trips, I noticed the husband shoving health and beauty products into his jacket. He did not see me and waved as he stood on line to pay for a few snacks he carried in his hand. Knowing the police were stationed at the tent on the side of the building, I went out and asked them to detain this man until I figured out what to do. As he left the store, the police grabbed him and threw him into the wall. They already had it figured out! As he hit the wall, all the stolen products fell to the floor along with a shiny handgun. The police had history with this man and I'm sure he had some with them. They promptly arrested him as I counted my blessings. I should have learned, from my vast experience, never trust the friendly ones.

Chapter 31-Live and Learn

Back in the supermarket , there was a very nice handicapped customer. He would come in to shop almost every day. "Hi John. How's the family?'" A telltale sign. After many "How's the family" days, I noticed he must have had a cat, or two, as he was stashing cat food and tuna cans under the cushion of his wheelchair. I followed him outside, stood in front of his chair and asked for my product to be returned. Of course he played stupid and I was losing my patience. In full view of the entire line of cashiers, and many customers waiting on their lines, I began to spin his chair in a state of delirium. As the chair spun faster, the cans began to fly out from under him. I stopped, picked up the cans and went back to work. Didn't see much of him after that. You would wonder why I would risk life and limb to protect something that was not mine. I often wonder the same thing. Speaking of cashiers, I had one of the sweetest older ladies working for me. Everyone loved and respected her. A male customer noticed she had made a mistake with his order and started to yell, curse, and belittle at her. He was in the midst of his rant when I sprang into action." Who the hell are you to speak to an older woman like that?'. I was about to lose it. His only reply to me was"I'm calling your boss". I had to respond with "Here's a quarter for the call". He had the balls to say "I'll take the quarter."! I had the balls to say" By the way you are dressed, you need the quarter. Now get the fuck out of my store!". A tremendous cheer rose from all the customers on line. They applauded me as this idiot hung his head and was about to leave. " I believe you owe this lady an apology". He apologized. "NOW get the fuck out"! Why is it always the loud mouths and the homeless. I spent countless days in court helping to convict shoplifters. The one who broke my heart was never charged. He was homeless and shoved a six pack of beer ,one can at a time, down his pant leg. The leg had a piece of rope around the bottom to prevent the cans from falling out. I followed him down the sidewalk as he left the store. I was calling after him to stop not realizing he was deaf.

I was able to convey to him that I wanted the beer back. He somehow understood and handed me one can. I shook my head NO and pointed at his pants. He handed me another, then another but was saving the last one for himself. As he began to walk away, with the last can, I stopped him. This is the part I am not that proud of. I took my box cutter out and tapped the can in his pants. It started spraying wildly as he shook his leg in an attempt to free the can. All I could say was "Enjoy that!". Not my finest hour. So, I consider all this experience as on the job training for the dollar store. I ended up opening a brand new store, in yes, another shitty neighborhood. Spent some time waiting for sales to increase. When they finally did, an opportunity arrived. My DM

was hard to read. Nice enough guy but I didn't trust him. He offered me a position as a field specialist. This was a fancy title allowing me to go to struggling stores to help them out of trouble. This was a good gig as these managers all made me, and my assistant, look better. Some of these stores were on the ground, meaning they were months behind in stocking the shelves or preparing for holidays. Remember, we all had staffing issues. Myself and Kevin, my assistant, would meet at a designated store and hopefully pull it together in an 8 hour period. It was easy for us. We didn't have to run a register or do any of the other hundred things these managers would have to do. We were Rock Stars. Everyone was thrilled to see us show up at their store. We were the help they needed and we were good!. I stayed in this position as many holiday's came and went.

The DM was happy with us and started to be more like a friend than the borderline psycho I thought he would be. It got to the point where we were filling in for vacations in various stores. One week here...one week there. This was a good gig until the corporation decided that one specialist is all they can afford. Kevin had seniority and frankly, failed in the past at being a manager. That left me going back into a store.I decided, once again, that this was not what I wanted to do,again.

Chapter 3-Me... Robbed?

The perfect ending to a week's vacation is receiving a prank call from the store at 10:05pm on the Sunday before I returned. "John, we were robbed!" Unfortunately this was no prank. Three armed men entered the store five minutes before closing. They had my assistant manager open the office safe. She was terrified, but not as much as the elderly cashier she had working with her.This poor woman was made to kneel on the floor as one of the thieves held his gun against the side of her head. The third assailant rounded up the few customers that were still shopping the aisles. He forced them to lie down on their bellies wherever he found them.When I arrived, the men had already left. The store was swarming with police and draped in crime scene tape. The office was left totally trashed with empty register tills thrown on the floor. The amount of fingerprint powder the police had used made it seem like a Christmas Hallmark card.These men were never caught. The store suffered a minor cash loss, afterall it was a dollar store. The elderly cashier was rushed to the hospital as she was clearly traumatized. We never heard from her again. The only other time I faced danger, I was alone in the store at 9am.Hard to believe! I had noticed a young man standing in the parking lot watching the store. The sunglasses and hoodie should have given him away but I really didn't expect trouble. He eventually entered the store and came up behind me.He tried to disguise his voice by speaking with a cheesy Spanish accent.He demanded the dinero. As I looked down at his hand, he was threatening me with a tiny pen knife that could have been mistaken for a nail clipper. This was his weapon of choice.I tried to reason with this idiot. I guess I felt bad for him. It was 9am. We were only open for an hour.How much dinero did he think I had? "Do you really want to go to prison for $22.00? This is armed robbery. I said that with a straight face. He pushed me aside, grabbed the few bills in the register and left. After the police responded to my 911 call, I was told this boy was wanted for 5 more robberies up and down the street. He was easily caught as he tried to rob number 6. I was called to testify in court. I have never been involved in the Grand Jury process and found it intimidating. I was waiting in a narrow hallway with the 5 other victims of this wannabe thug. When called, we each entered the courtroom through a door at the end of this hall. The door led to a raised platform that contained a single chair. You came face to face with an audience of 50 people waiting to hear your story. If I knew I had to perform, I would have prepared. Bottom line, he was sentenced, I had two weeks off with pay, and made 5 friends.

Chapter 33-What Future?

I met with the DM and told him I would accept retirement before I accepted his decision to put me back into a store."Why would you want to retire"? I quickly and nastily answered with "Because I can and you can't!" He panicked and offered me a part time specialist position. That, along with Social Security, would keep me active and I would be able to get a weekly paycheck. First, there was no such job as a part time specialist. He was planning on leaving me full time. He was playing a dangerous game which could cost him his job.I later found out he was planning to leave. He didn't care! I applied for Social Security and started collecting when I turned 62. With the SSA, at 62 you could only earn 15K for the year. As I tried to keep my hours to a minimum, this and that would always happen. I heard the phrase "Do me a favor" at least once a week. My first year of collecting put me over my limit by six thousand dollars! Surprise...you have to pay that back! The second year, I still did not learn, and earned three thousand over. This made it nearly impossible to consider living on my monthly retirement . The job in Carolina wiped out my 401K, but we had nice furniture. The pension from the kosher store was renegotiated after the company went out of business. The 10 years that I invested in the union became 15 years to qualify. With retirement dreams turning into nightmares, I needed a new plan.

Chapter 34-The Final Countdown

My wife, son, and daughter were all working together in a specialty store. This was a high end store belonging to a small chain that was located in only the upscale neighborhoods. They would specialize in gourmet foods, catering, and store made everything. This store, by some ungodly reason, was managed by a former manager in the kosher chain. I knew him for years. My family would joke about me asking him for a job. I was attempting to live on my retirement pittance and had no intention of starting with a new company now. I decided to apply for a part time position. A few hours a week just for something to do.This was at the start of the pandemic. They needed full time help as any help was limited to the healthy. The store was emptying out faster than we could fill it and days turned into weeks of full time hours. By now, I no longer had to fear making too much money. The government grants forgiveness to those of us over 65. I was still not happy having to work this many hours,but the money was nice. The ironic thing was that the store smelled of cheese the moment you walked in. I detest cheese in any form. Had for years. My family would joke with me as to my getting past the smell to ever work there. I pushed ahead. A new company incentive reared its head. Each store was to hire a manager for the grocery department. Up until now, this was the responsibility of one of the two assistant managers in each building. I was already doing the job so the incentive for me was the fat raise they offered. I ultimately interviewed and was awarded the position. Salaried again with less time at home than at work. A specialty store cannot compete with a supermarket on any level. We were overpriced and offered little in the way of grocery variety. I gave it my best but was constantly butting heads with the assistant who couldn't let go. I may sound bitter at this point but remember that I had this same position when I was 19, and it meant something. During an argument with one of the assistants, I crafted the phrase "The day you were born, I already had 45 years experience"! Old school has no place in this modern day and age.Now, the only experience that counts is the person's ability to kiss ass. My newly concocted plan for the future of my family is to drop dead at work leaving them over a million dollars in insurance payouts.I would like to leave you with a parting thought...Life continues to provide the exaggerations. I am thankful for that! YA MUDDAS!